It's a Dog's New York

It's a Dog's New York

Susan L. Roth

NATIONAL GEOGRAPHIC SOCIETY
WASHINGTON, D.C.

To Pepper, ...and to Boo, Chef, Ninja, and Suivante Adams-Athanassakis; Pete Adler; Kirby and Trapper Altholz; Rusty Batelle; Brutus and Hecate Cahnmann; Pajtas Carleton; Bobo Castle-Baron and Monkey Castle; Dinah Domini; Cider, Mollie, and Truffle Drachman; Brit, Jesse, and Juliet Eakin; Poochie Erickson; The Bunyips Fex; Caleb and Chaucer Gorden; Brownie Harvey; Meagan Hoffman; Amigo Laufer; Babe, Bonnie, Ginger, and Kelly McFarlane; Clean, Cortu, Dea, Natalina, Taddeo, Wanda (and Michele-the-Cat) Muggeo; Annie and Maggie Patz; Felix Pfeiffer; Polo Phang; Homewood and Pongo Rodowsky; Morgan, Poppy, and Samantha Willoughby DeKalb Lafayette Roth; Poochie Roth; Cassie Schwartz; Saki Shuldiner; Caesar Simmons; and Fendel Yale.

But **NOT** to DRUSESS, the mean dog who bit Pepper's sister.

Acknowledgments: I wish to thank Julia Bergman; Donald Carlin of Village 1 Hour Photo, Whitestone, NY; Nancy Laties Feresten; Nina Hoffman; Bea Jackson; Jeannette Larsen; Martin Laufer; Beverly Maiorana and Susan Pedersen of The Minuteman Press, Great Neck, NY; Joan Pappas; Nancy Patz; Ruth Phang; Barbara Ann Porte; Alex Roth; Robert Salazar; Jim Field, Ann Schultz and Bow Wag Kennels; Jill Oriane Tarlau; and Sheri Walter of the Queens Borough Public Library, Whitestone, NY. And a double thank you to Barbara Ann Porte who not only gave me the gift of friendship, but also the gift of new friends: the writers and illustrators group of Long Island. And a special thank you to all of them for being so welcoming. And even more than as always, AAA, ETL, JR.

Special thanks to Sol Steinmetz, New York linguist and lexicographer extraordinaire, who has edited many dictionaries, most recently the Random House Webster's College Dictionary, for carefully reviewing and correcting the spelling of Rover's accent.

About the illustrations, by Rover

Look, don't get any ideas, awright? The awt in this book is NOT compuda-generated. Susan L. Rawth couldn't draw a compuda-generated piece of awt with a rula. These pitchas were made with huh scissas and huh Brownie camera, a few culla copies, and a few random leftovas from huh pay-pa collection. Who says ya can't make good awt anymua without a compuda?

How to read this book, by Rover

Read this book just the way it looks and ya'll sound just like a New Yawka!

A note about the text, by Pepper

NEW New Yorkers sometimes need simultaneous translations to understand when OLD New Yorkers are talking. In this book the editor decided to help out with translations of the harder words. She figured since I'm here to stay, that I could work on the easier words myself. I'm getting better at it already.

As for the rest of the story, they left one thing out: I especially miss the air-conditioning vent on the floor in the kitchen of the old house because when it was really hot the cold air used to blow on my belly when I sat on top of it.

Library of Congress Cataloging-in-Publication Data

Roth, Susan L.
It's a dog's New York / By Susan L. Roth.
p. cm.
Summary: Pepper is sad about moving to New York City until he meets a neighbor who thinks the biggest city anywhere is also the best city when you're a dog.
ISBN 0-7922-7054-1 (hard cover)
[1. New York (N.Y.)—Fiction. 2. Dogs—Fiction. 3. Moving, Household—Fiction.} I. Title.
PZ7.R737 It 2001
[E]—dc21   00-012760

The world's largest nonprofit scientific and educational organization, the National Geographic Society was founded in 1888 "for the increase and diffusion of geographic knowledge." Since then it has supported scientific exploration and spread information to its more than eight million members worldwide. The National Geographic Society educates and inspires millions every day through magazines, books, television programs, videos, maps and atlases, research grants, the National Geographic Bee, teacher workshops, and innovative classroom materials. The Society is supported through membership dues, charitable donations, and income from the sale of its educational products. Members receive NATIONAL GEOGRAPHIC magazine—the Society's official journal—discounts on Society products and other benefits. For more information about the National Geographic Society, its educational programs and publications, and ways to support its work, please call 1-800-NGS-LINE (647-5463) or write to the following address:

National Geographic Society

1145 17th Street N.W.
Washington, D.C. 20036-4688
U.S.A.

Visit the Society's Web site: www.nationalgeographic.com

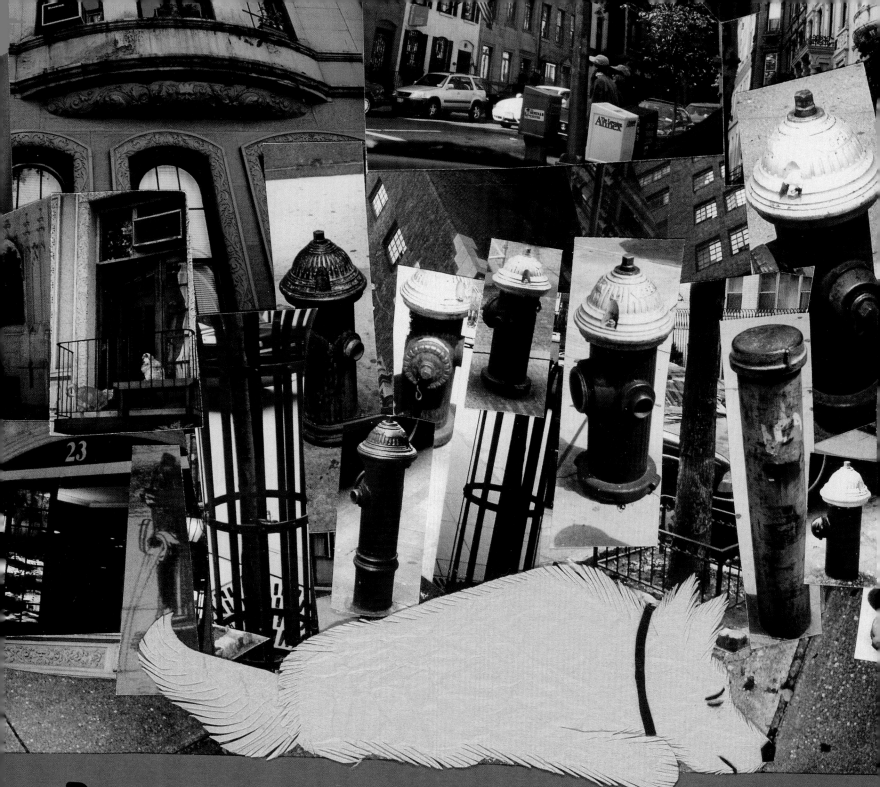

Pepper sat on the sidewalk remembering the time before he moved. He remembered the beech tree in his big backyard. He remembered his blue doghouse, shaped like an igloo. He remembered his friend Brutus, who lived down the street. Pepper lowered his chin onto his paw. He shut his eyes. It was a beautiful day in New York City, but Pepper didn't care—until the dog next door started talking.

"Don't TELL me!" said the dog next door.
"I KNOW why ya so sad. Ya homesick. I've seen sad dawgs like you befua. Listen ta me, ya like chasin pigeons, AM I RIGHT?" Pepper lifted his ears. "I KNEW IT!" said the dog next door. "Welcome ta New Yawk!"

"I'm ya new nay-ba. What's ya name?" asked the dog next door.

"Pepper."

"Peppa? ROVA! Gimme ya paw, Peppa! Like I was sayin, New Yawk has pigeons. Ya take the ellevayda up ta the top of the Empawya State Building, you're in pigeon city! We don't call em sky scrapas fa nothin! I'll go up with ya any time."

"Well, maybe some day," said Pepper.

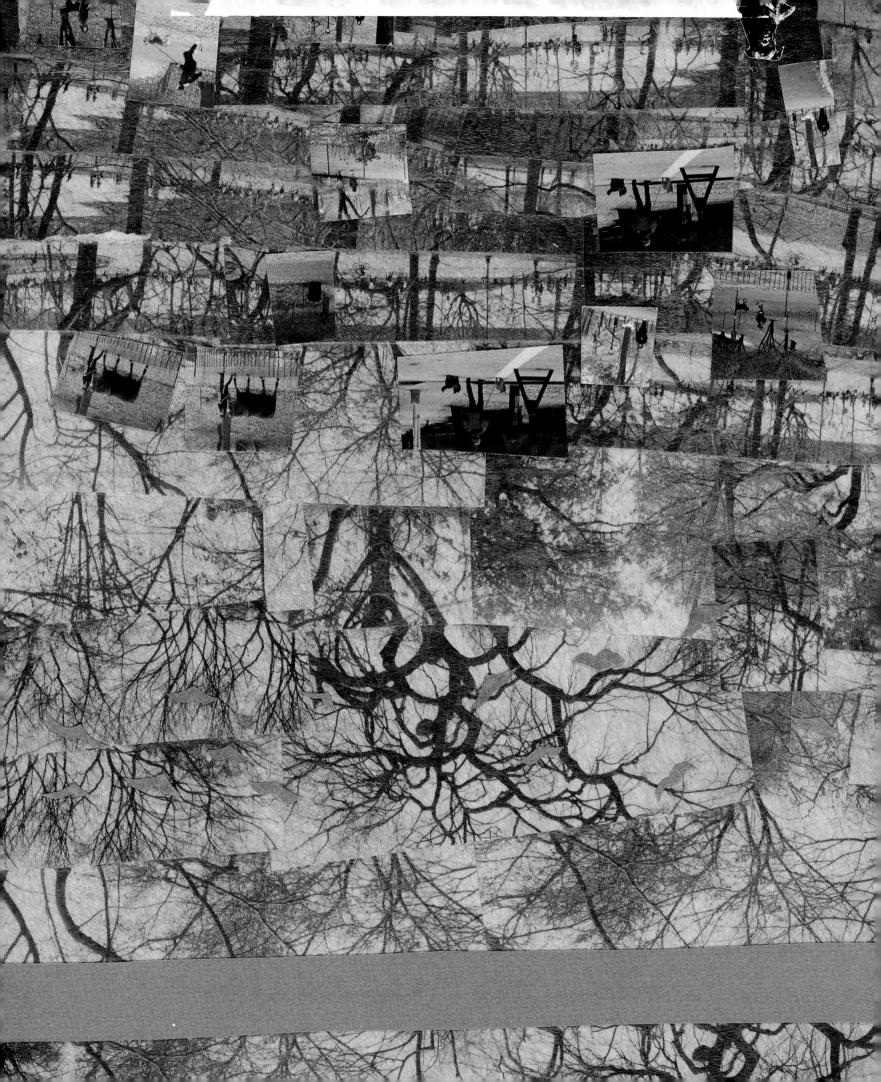

"Ya wan company," said Rover, "you'll go ta Cenchral Pawk. There's plenny a dawgs. I'll introduce ya ta everybody. There's grass ta run on, dirt ta dig in, gawbidge cans ta knock ova, you name it. Pigeons, too, as a matta a fact. It's a great place."

"Hmmmm," said Pepper.

"Now, ya HAFTA see Rock-a-fella Centa. In the winta EVERYBODY goes ta slide on the ice. Ya fall down, then everybody wants ta pet ya. They'll scratch ya ears, they'll rub ya belly. It's not a pawk, but there's still plenny a room. Who says The City is nothin but sawydwauks?"

"That's what I used to think," said Pepper.

"Hah!" said Rover.

"Ya thirsty? Ya wanna drink? There's a big pool fulla wauda right in front of the MetroPOLlitan Museum of Awt." Pepper picked up his head.

"That sounds all right," he said.

"I'll tell you what sounds BETTA!" said Rover.

"CAWNAGEE HOALL! Ya like music? I neva met a dawg who didn't like music. ASK ME HOWDA GET TA CAWNAGEE HOALL!"

"What?" said Pepper.

"Go on. Say, 'HOW DA YA GET TA CAWNAGEE HOALL.'"

"How do you get to Carnegie Hall?"

"YA HAFTA PRACTICE!" howled Rover. "GET IT?"

"That's a good one," said Pepper.

"NOW ya bawking," said Rover. "If ya tired a sight-seein..."

"...you'll bawk at the law-yins!"

"Come on," said Pepper.

"You'll see," said Rover. "The New Yawk Public Lawy-bry has ten million books! Somebody hasta gawd em."

"I wouldn't bark at a lion," said Pepper. "A lion could eat you up."

"Take it easy," said Rover. "Not these law-yins."

"On TV, last New Year's Eve at midnight, did ya see the big boall drop?"

"Of course I did," said Pepper.

"Ya know that was right here in Tawymz Squay-a? We can go there any-time. If we go next New Year's Eve, all ya old friends'll be watchin YOU!

"No kidding?" said Pepper.

"WOULD I LIE TA YA?" said Rover. "Now tell me. Ya hungry?"

"If ya hungry, we'll go ta Coney Awylind. I know a great place to eat dawgs."

"Eat what!?" said Pepper.

"Not DAWG dawgs, country boy. I mean HOT dawgs. You know, franks, HOT dawgs, weenez."

"We have hot dogs, too!" said Pepper. He sniffed the air and licked his chops. "We used to cook them in the backyard at home."

"Peppa, home is where the hawt is. And besides, NOTHIN beats a New Yawk dawg!"

"And after that we'll take the Staten Awylind Ferry. You'll have the wind on ya fuh, the smell of the sea, the rock of the boat. Ya'll see the Sta-chew a Libba-dee! Ya gonna LOVE it!"

Pepper stood up. "Maybe I will," he said, stretching.

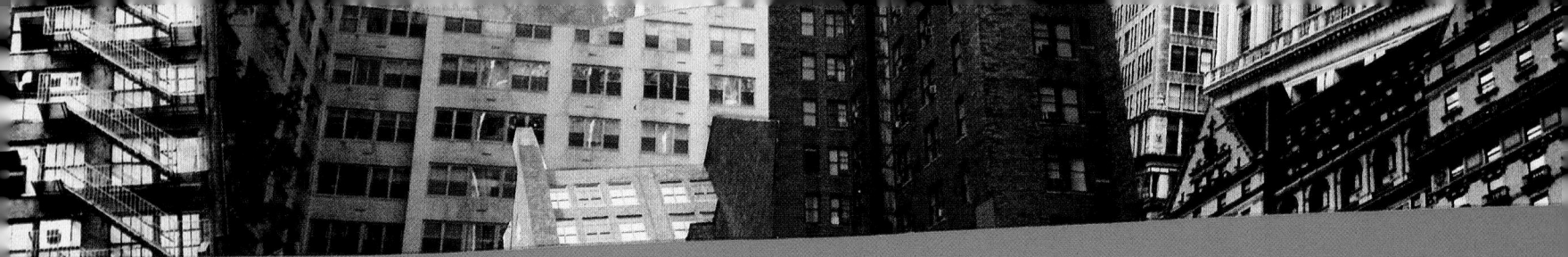

"Hold it, Peppa," said Rover. "I've got a little somethin fer ya. Now rememba, New Yawk has great bones if ya know where ta dig!"

"Thank you!" said Pepper.

"Fuh-GEDDA-bow-dit," said Rover. "But DON'T f'get I'm ya nay-ba. Ya have a friend here. I've had my rabies shots, even if I don't sound like it. So. Ya wanna stawt the tua?"

Pepper shook himself. His ears were up. He wagged his tail. "Let's go!" said Pepper.

forget about it

start the tour

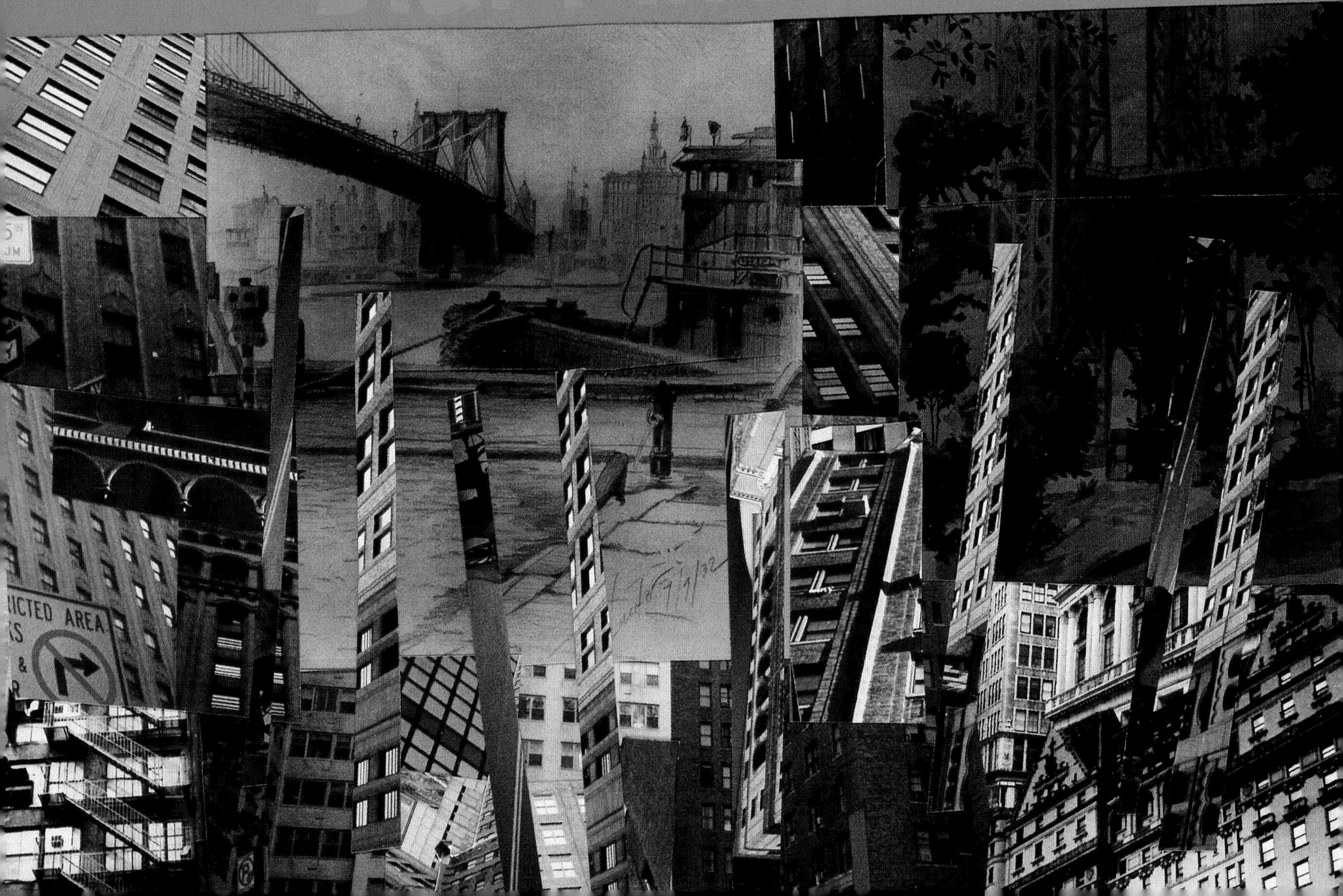

And they did.

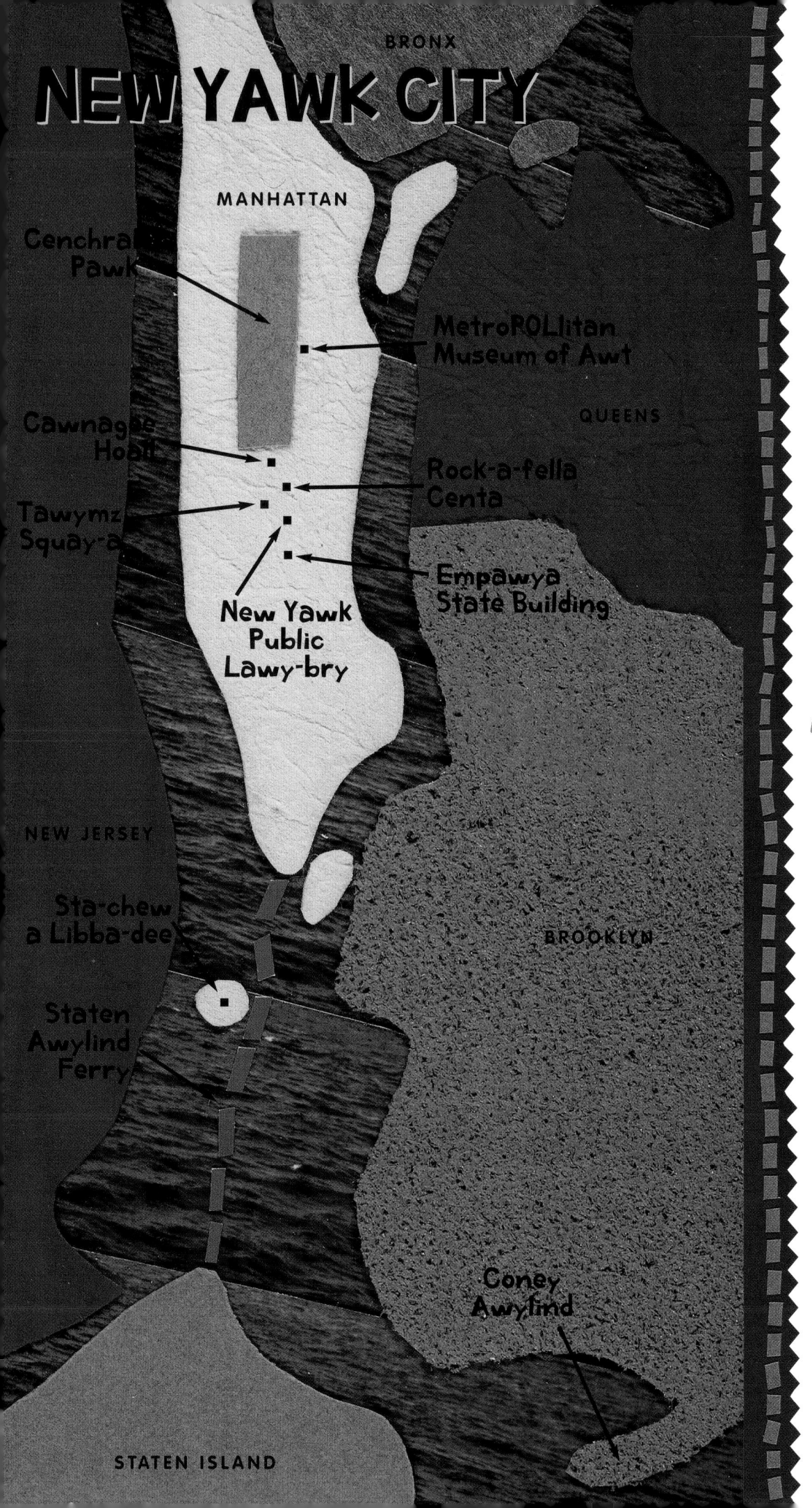

NEW YAWK CITY

NEW YORK CITY

Empawya State Building
EMPIRE STATE BUILDING

Cenchral Pawk
CENTRAL PARK

Rock-a-fella Centa
ROCKEFELLER CENTER

MetroPOLlitan Museum of Awt
METROPOLITAN MUSEUM OF ART

Cawnagee Hoall
CARNEGIE HALL

New Yawk Public Lawy-bry
NEW YORK PUBLIC LIBRARY

Tawymz Squay-a
TIMES SQUARE

Coney Awylind
CONEY ISLAND

Staten Awylind Ferry
STATEN ISLAND FERRY

Sta-chew a Libba-dee
STATUE OF LIBERTY